# ROCK, Rosetta, ROCK!

# ROLL, Rosetta, ROLL!

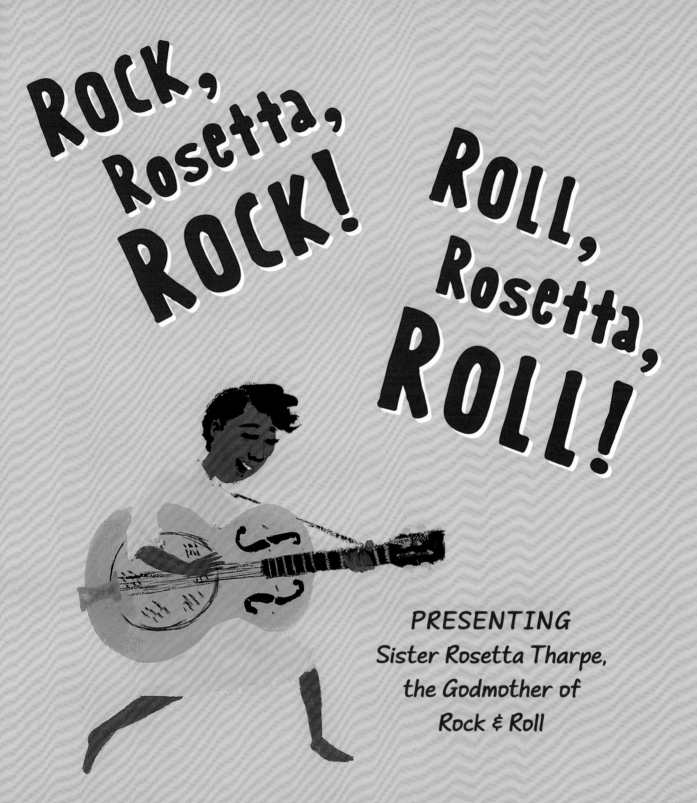

**PRESENTING**
Sister Rosetta Tharpe,
the Godmother of
Rock & Roll

Written by **TONYA BOLDEN**

Illustrated by **R. GREGORY CHRISTIE**

**HARPER**
*An Imprint of HarperCollinsPublishers*

# Rock, Rosetta, Rock!
## Roll, Rosetta, Roll!

A long, long time ago, there you were.

Pint-size sensation in tiny
Cotton Plant, Arkansas.

Rosa,

Rosabell,

Rosie Etta.

Who had a clue you'd one
day rock the world?

Little girl.
**Big guitar.**

Music in your air,
in your hair,
in your bones,
wiggling your toes.

Making downright mighty
music, music, **music.**

Tiny digits of your hands
    skipping,
        strumming,
            strolling,                     up
                rolling         and
                                    down

        that big guitar's fingerboard.

## Rock, Rosetta, Rock!
## Roll, Rosetta, Roll!

Then up jumped the day Mama had a
strong-strong calling to quit your tiny town,
be a preacher,
take your genius with her,
let it shine, let it shine in a bigger place,
a wider space!

You zooped into your travelin' shoes
for a choo-choo up to Chicago.

There, in that big, bustling place on the shore of a great lake,
you became a wonder in a Fortieth Street church.

A star!

At outdoor revivals, on street corners—wherever Mama preached—
you *played, played, played,* moving folks to clap happy,
stamp their feet,
shout, holler—toss coins too!
Jump for joy over your mighty music, music, music.

You put so much heart and soul—
such power—
into
songs of worship,
songs of praise.

Little girl.
**Big guitar.**
Smile so "alive," remembered one lady.

Little girl.
**Big guitar.**

Too, you had a mighty amount of singing in your soul, yes you did.

Little girl.
## Big voice.

Belting out the rhythm-bound Gospel sound,
songs born in the souls of Black folk about
good news even in grim times.

Songs like "Up Above My Head, I Hear Music in the Air."

With music in your air,

in your hair,

in your bones,

wiggling your toes—

that travelin' bag sure stayed packed.

All grown, you took Gospel
music far beyond the walls, the
halls of this and that church.

You gifted Gospel music big-time
to people all over the place!

Mixing it up with beats from Gospel's
Cousin Boogie-Woogie,
Cousin Jazz,
Cousin Swing,
Cousin the big, bad Blues.

Playing and singing the Lord's songs in a nightclub?

Lots of church folk frowned, shook their heads at that.

But you believed it was right—
*and* righteous—
to play wherever you pleased.
And you did it like nobody else!

With those flying fingers of
yours, they said you made
a guitar *talk!*

On Decca discs,
all over the States,
across the ocean blue,
on radio,
TV . . .

You *played, played, played*–and *sang!*
as the fabulous,
flamboyant
Sister Rosetta Tharpe!

Rock, Rosetta, Rock!
Roll, Rosetta, Roll!

Sister
ROSETTA

That lively smile still dazzling like diamonds.

Rhinestone earrings shaped like guitars.

You were a great entertainer prone to stopping mid-song,
flipping folks a joke,
beguiling them with an angelic pose,
blowing them away with a kickin' guitar solo.

Bold,
audacious—
in a word, *bodacious*,
whatever the song.

Be it your old favorite, "Up Above My Head, I Hear Music in the Air," or

"Singing in My Soul," about peace and joy, or

"This Train," about a choo-choo to a place of glory.

And—ooh!—there was your "Rock Me,"
about a strong-strong longing to be cradled in a

whole

lot of

LOVE.

With big bands,
solo,
as half of a duet,
with quartets,

You *played, played, played*–and *sang!*

(Jammed on the piano too!)

Meanwhile lots of younger cats—some future legends—
had been goin' *wow-wow* wild over you.

Diggin' your licks.
Coppin' your style.

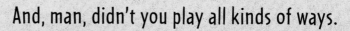

And, man, didn't you play all kinds of ways.

Up on your toes!
Down on the floor!
Behind your back!

Stepping!

Striding!

Stomping!

Jumping up onstage—
in high heels at that!

Hip-hugging your guitar.

Duckwalking it too!

You even rocked fans in the English rain.

Sister Rosetta Tharpe,
with all your
fiery-fierce-feisty picking and plucking,
you blazed a trail for a fast-paced,
hard-driving, gritty, gutsy sound that made
the electric guitar
a star.

A music called Rock & Roll.

Rock, Rosetta, Rock!
Roll, Rosetta, Roll!

# TIMELINE

**March 20, 1915** – Rosetta is born in Cotton Plant, Arkansas, to farmworkers Katie Harper and Willis (or Willie) Atkins. Both are fine singers and play musical instruments. Mama plays the mandolin and the piano; Papa, the harmonica and guitar.

**1921** – Rosetta begins performing solo at Chicago's Church of God in Christ (COGIC), now Roberts Temple COGIC, at Fortieth and South State Streets. She will go on to perform at other places in and outside Chicago.

**November 17, 1934** – Marries COGIC preacher Thomas Tharpe. Over the next few years, the couple makes southern Florida their base, and they become a successful act—with her singing and playing guitar and him preaching. They become regulars at COGIC's Miami Temple, now A.M. Cohen Temple COGIC. Because the church's Sunday services are broadcast on radio, Rosetta's sound reaches a wide audience.

**1938** – Having left her husband, Rosetta becomes a hit at New York City's famous Cotton Club, then located in midtown Manhattan (and for white patrons only). Superstars performing there include the wild and crazy bandleader Cab Calloway. Rosetta's triumph at the Cotton Club leads to gigs at other top spots, such as Harlem's Apollo Theater.

**October 31, 1938** – Rosetta cuts her first records—four sides for Decca Records. "Rock Me" is one of the songs.

**December 23, 1938** – At New York City's fabulous Carnegie Hall, Rosetta performs in a groundbreaking concert: From Spirituals to Swing, a celebration of Black contributions to music and song. Other greats on the bill include the jazz luminary Count Basie.

**1941** – Rosetta begins performing religious and secular songs with Lucky Millinder's sensational band—first at Harlem's legendary Savoy Ballroom, then out on the road.

**1943** – Rosetta steps out into a solo career. Also, she divorces Thomas Tharpe and marries promoter and booking agent Foch Allen.

**September 26, 1944** – With forty recordings under her belt, Rosetta cuts four more sides. One of them, "Strange Things Happening Every Day," about religious hypocrites, becomes a big hit. It is the first gospel song to cross over and make it onto *Billboard* magazine's R&B chart (then called the Race Records chart). In April 1945, the song held the number-two spot on that chart. Some music historians consider Rosetta's rendition of "Strange Things" the first rock & roll record.

**1946** – Rosetta teams up with another gospel singer, contralto Marie Knight. Rambunctious Rosetta and regal-looking Marie tour widely and make a number of records together. They will split up in 1949, but they remain friends and perform (and record) together later.

**May 15, 1950** – Rosetta embarks on a national tour with her backup singers, the Rosettes; her pianist and musical director,

James Roots Jr.; and Mama, a great gospel singer in her own right. According to one newspaper, Rosetta's gospel caravan is set to give 101 concerts over the course of 115 days in 97 cities.

July 3, 1951 – Having divorced Foch Allen in 1947, Rosetta marries Russell Morrison (who will become her manager) in one of the most over-the-top wedding ceremonies of the century. It is held at Griffith Stadium in Washington, DC, before a crowd of about twenty thousand. Marie Knight is her maid of honor, and the Rosettes are her bridesmaids. Rosetta's outfit includes a white scoop-neck dress with a five-foot train, a rhinestone- and pearl-studded tiara, and a sequin-trimmed veil. After the ceremony, Rosetta headlines a concert that includes the Harmonizing Four of Richmond. The spectacle ends with an amazing fireworks display, including an image of Rosetta strumming a guitar!

November 19, 1957 – Rosetta heads overseas. First stop: Britain, where she performs in more than a dozen cities.

November 22, 1957 – London's *Daily Mirror* publishes a piece on Rosetta in which she is quoted as saying, "All this new stuff they call rock 'n' roll, why, I've been playing that for years now." By the time she returns to the States in fall 1958, Rosetta will have performed in France, Germany, and several other European nations.

Spring 1964 – Rosetta heads overseas again, to Britain, as part of the American Folk, Blues, and Gospel Caravan.

May 7, 1964 – Granada Television produces the musical special *Blues and Gospel Train*, staged in an abandoned Manchester train station made to look like one in the American South. And on this rainy day, Rosetta's opener is a rousing rendition of "Didn't It Rain." In this show, which includes the great blues singer-songwriter and guitarist Muddy Waters, she also performs "He's Got the Whole World in His Hands." When Granada Television airs the concert in August, twelve million people tune in.

1968 – Mama dies. Also this year, Rosetta learns that she has diabetes.

1970 – Rosetta suffers a stroke.

1971 – Due to complications from diabetes, one of Rosetta's legs is amputated.

July 26, 1972 – Rosetta performs at New York City's Lincoln Center as part of a twelve-day Black arts festival, Soul at the Center. This is her last major appearance.

October 9, 1973 – Sister Rosetta Tharpe dies in Philadelphia at age fifty-eight following another stroke, just before she was to record an album. She is buried in an unmarked grave in Philadelphia's Northwood Cemetery.

January 11, 2008 – Marie Knight, then in her eighties, along with other great performers, holds what one paper calls "a gospel extravaganza" in honor of Rosetta at Philadelphia's Keswick Theatre. The concert raises money for a rose granite headstone for Rosetta's grave.

# AUTHOR'S NOTE

When Sister Rosetta Tharpe started doing her thing, it was pretty rare to see a girl (or a woman) strum-strum-strumming away on guitar.

Clearly Rosetta wasn't fazed by the thinking that the guitar (like the saxophone and drums) was a man's instrument.

"Can't no man play like me," she later declared. "I play better than a man." And Rosetta was not exaggerating. Her picking and plucking on an acoustic or electric guitar were the stuff of legend.

This bold soul, who largely lived life on her own terms, was anything but conventional and ordinary.

She married three times and, they say, had romances with more than a few women.

At one point she made beaucoup bucks.

At one point she went broke.

For most of her career, Rosetta had to put up with segregation. When she was on the road, she couldn't rest her head or have a meal just anywhere she pleased. Many hotels and restaurants all over the United States refused to have Black guests.

Through it all, Rosetta *played, played, played* —and *sang!*, becoming a great inspiration to future music legends.

These legends include the leg-shaking, hip-swiveling, hip-swinging singer-guitarist Elvis Presley, often called the King of Rock & Roll.

Sister Rosetta Tharpe also had a major influence on the duck-walking singer-songwriter-guitarist Chuck Berry and on the flashy singer-songwriter-piano-player Little Richard.

And there was the country, gospel, folk, blues, rockabilly, and rock & roll singer-songwriter-guitarist Johnny Cash. When Cash was inducted into the Rock & Roll Hall of Fame in 1992, he spoke of Rosetta's impact on him in his acceptance speech: "It was at the Home of the Blues record shop [in Memphis, Tennessee] where I bought my first recording of Sister Rosetta Tharpe singing those great gospel songs." Cash said that some of his early songs "were influenced by people like Sister Rosetta Tharpe."

The many women Rosetta influenced include the great gospel and R & B singer Aretha Franklin, hailed as the Queen of Soul.

After Rosetta died, for years a host of folks didn't know that she had ever existed, didn't know what a phenomenal, blow-'em-away talent she was.

But then, don't you know, the lady had a comeback—became a star again!

In 2003, MC Records released the album *Shout, Sister, Shout! A Tribute to Sister Rosetta Tharpe.* Four years later came the biography *Shout, Sister, Shout! The Untold Story of Rock-and-Roll Trailblazer Sister Rosetta Tharpe* by historian Gayle F. Wald, who had written the liner notes for that tribute album. It was also in 2007 that Rosetta was inducted into the Blues Hall of Fame.

And the recognition kept coming!

In 2011, the documentary *The Godmother of Rock & Roll: Sister Rosetta Tharpe,* directed by Mick Csáky, premiered in the UK, then, in 2013, in the United States on PBS as an episode on *American Masters.*

A few years later, in 2018—more than forty years after her death—Sister Rosetta Tharpe was inducted into the Rock & Roll Hall of Fame, in the category of Early Influences. Two Black women guitarists—Brittany Howard and Felicia Collins—did the honors of inducting her.

And Sister Rosetta Tharpe, once a little girl with a big guitar, has continued to influence musicians and singers down to this very day!

# SOURCES

## NARRATIVE
11 **"alive":** Gayle F. Wald, *Shout, Sister, Shout! The Untold Story of Rock-and-Roll Trailblazer Sister Rosetta Tharpe.* (Boston: Beacon Press, 2007), page 2.

## TIMELINE
37 **Extent of 1950 national tour:** "Sister Tharpe Gospel Caravan Set for Tour." *Norfolk Journal and Guide,* May 6, 1950, page D20.

37 **"All this new stuff they call rock 'n' roll . . .":** Wald, *Shout, Sister, Shout!,* page 184.

37 **"gospel extravaganza":** Nick Cristiano, "Benefit to Ring with the Memory of a Gospel Great," *Philadelphia Inquirer,* January 11, 2008, page W18.

## AUTHOR'S NOTE
38 **"Can't no man . . . better than a man":** Pat Monroe, "Sister Rosetta Tharpe: Godmother of Rock & Roll," *Edinburgh Music Review,* January 31, 2021, www.edinburghmusicreview.com/blog/sister-rosetta-tharpe-godmother-of-rock-amp-roll.

38 **"It was at the Home of the Blues record shop . . . like Sister Rosetta Tharpe":** Marissa Lorusso, "How One of Music's Biggest Stars Almost Disappeared, and How Her Legacy Was Saved." NPR, September 27, 2019, www.npr.org/2019/09/27/759601364/how-one-of-musics-biggest-stars-almost-disappeared-and-how-her-legacy-was-saved.

For Gayle F. Wald
—T.B.

For the sharecroppers, enslaved and creative souls
who used music, dancing, and singing to find joyful
humanity within a  bittersweet life.
—R.G.C.

Rock, Rosetta, Rock! Roll, Rosetta, Roll!
Text copyright © 2023 by Tonya Bolden
Illustrations copyright © 2023 by R. Gregory Christie
All rights reserved. Manufactured in Italy.
No part of this book may be used or reproduced in any manner whatsoever without written permission except
in the case of brief quotations embodied in critical articles and reviews. For information address HarperCollins
Children's Books, a division of HarperCollins Publishers, 195 Broadway, New York, NY 10007.
www.harpercollinschildrens.com

Library of Congress Control Number: 2021951265
ISBN 978-0-06-299438-7

The artist used acryla gouache on illustration board to create the illustrations for this book.
Typography by Rachel Zegar

22 23 24 25 26  RTLO  10 9 8 7 6 5 4 3 2 1
First Edition